DRIVING IS

INDEPE

for thos

Specific Needs

John P Brown (Cert. Ed. Cert. Sp. Ed. Cert. Disability. ADI)
Specialist Teacher and Disability Driving Instructor

Revised 2016

Published by: Driving is --- Publications. 6 BH21 2SR

Printed by: Think Ink.

ISBN 978-0-9558282-6-3

CONTENTS

Feel free to use the individual chapters as a basis for discussion. If you wish for further information re the books, then please refer to my web site:- www.drivingincludesu.co.uk

BOOK 1 'Driving is more about Psychology than Systems'. (revised 2009 / 2012)

BOOK 2 'Driving is Turning Disability into Ability'.

BOOK 3 'Driving is Independence for those with Specific Needs'. (revised 2016)

BOOK 4 'Driving is Challenging and Important for Older Drivers'.

BOOK 5 'Driving is Overcoming Dyspraxia'.

John P Brown. (July. 2016)

i) Terminology

Special Needs (SN): a generic description of any aspect of Physical, Mental, Emotional and Educational Difficulties.

Specific Needs (SpN): used for normally well-functioning people whose development may have varied from the norm, or who have experienced specific areas of difficulty which may make them need to learn in an alternative way which focuses and builds on their strengths.

Complex Needs: the requirements necessary for inter-related conditions, which may have developed from one root cause. Dyslexia may be linked to ADHD and Aspergers may be linked with Dyspraxia, but through consequent frustration, these may lead to socially unacceptable behaviour. The difficulty for teachers is to be able to work out what the underlying root cause is, rather than just reacting to what they are observing.

Specific Requirements: a term used to explain the appropriate support which would help balance the differences to make sure the clients are not disadvantaged and so are able to attain their natural potential.

Inclusion: this was the term used in the 1978 Warnock Report into Special Educational Needs, which meant that legally children with SN must be given the same educational opportunities. *"Inclusion should mean being involved in a common enterprise of learning."* This did not necessarily mean they had to be taught in the same way or even at the same level, but that they should be **included** and provided with all relevant opportunities, rather than being excluded and unable to attain success in the same way as their peers.

Statement: the term used under the 1981 Education Act to describe the legal document which 'States' the requirements of children in education whose needs are severe enough to be assessed and to have LEA provision.

Education Health & Care Plans: These have replaced Statements.

Access : the different ways that must be used to enable those with Specific Needs to take part in normal education and social activities.

Differentiation: the term used to explain the changes which must be made to help the student achieve the results they are capable of attaining. Differentiation can be divided into three sections.

1. **Content:** through different ways of **Presentation.**
2. **Process:** through employing different teaching **Methods.**
3. **Assessment:** through enabling them to demonstrate in different ways their new **Knowledge**.

It does not mean 'dumbing-down', but finding more appropriate methods to achieve the same level of success.

Spectrum The condition is so termed since there is a huge variation in both the manifestation and in the degree of effect and affect it can have. If mild and difficult to pin-point, then the term **tendencies** may also be used, e.g. Autistic Spectrum Disorder or Autistic Tendencies.

Who is Affected? 21% of the population will have some area of diagnosed Special Need, but only a few of those receive Statements so the majority will have Hidden Disabilities. At least half of those diagnosed will never be able to drive, nor would they expect to, but many more with undiagnosed Specific Needs will wish to learn and could become safe competent drivers. We can estimate that 20% who wish to learn to drive will have Specific Needs which should be understood and catered for. Many of those hidden difficulties will never have been identified, nor would the learner drivers wish to be categorised as having Special Needs.

Identified or Recognised? If it was suggested candidates had a SN they could be seriously insulted as many of them will have been academically capable and developed successful coping strategies or will have learnt to mask their problems. It would therefore be unwise to either ask them, or to imply they have a problem unless they volunteer the information, but it is still important that their needs are recognised and differentiation in both teaching and assessment is implemented.

If they were given an option to use the methods they actually employ to drive independently and were given the choice to be assessed on their strengths, it would not devalue the integrity of the tests because the same knowledge would be being assessed, but by using different methods. The instructor needs to be sensitive to their client's needs and to work in partnership with them to develop their strengths and the examiner needs to understand their behaviour in order to correctly judge their driving ability.

ii) **Should ADIs Diagnose?**

I was contacted by an irate mother who asked me to assess and teach her daughter following her current instructor's diagnosis of 'autism.' I calmed her down by explaining that I believed her daughter may benefit from a different form of teaching and after giving a few pointers and directed help she soon began to enjoy her lessons and became a proficient driver without any sign of autistic traits.

It is possible for ADIs to actually 'create' what can appear to be Special Needs if they teach in an inappropriate way for that particular client. It could also be argued that a few Examiners can also 'create' failure if they do not recognise or understand the candidate's condition, or the reasons which lie beneath the techniques they employ to assist their safe-driving.

I can assure readers that this is not an attack on instructors or examiners, but that we should consider if our methods are actually making the situation worse. I deeply respect the examiners with whom I work as they are highly experienced and sympathetic to those with Specific Needs, but with more knowledge and training, some situations could be avoided.

When applying for a test, it is difficult to know what should be declared if the client does not know, or will not recognise, or wants to keep quiet that they have a Specific Need. ADIs are not medics and we should not be put in the position of having to 'diagnose'. We should just state **what they require,** rather than have to diagnose a formal condition.

I taught a young dancer with 'Cerebral Palsy,' but the booking department wanted to register her as having a mobility disability, rather than the manifest **Information Processing** problem, which was not on their list of disabilities, so we had to settle for Dyspraxia and a disability slot!!

What I wanted to be able to state was; *"This candidate will take time to understand your directions, so please point to reinforce them and give them clearly and in good time to enable her to listen, comprehend and carry them out."*

The on-line application has improved enormously, but I now also give the examiner a card stating **what the candidate requires** rather than state a named condition. It is in the lap of the gods as to whether they understand the significance of the declared conditions and I feel uncomfortable when they ask the candidate, *"you have declared a disability, so what modifications do* *you need to the car?"* In the mind of the candidate they have not declared a 'disability,' but only a **'difficulty'** which may require extra time and understanding. The card removes the embarrassment of explaining, because spoken words are not needed, but the message has still been conveyed.

When ID was first introduced, a lot of mistakes were made by examiners who strictly followed their procedure and chose the task they thought was the most appropriate, rather than seeking from the candidate what they required and so mistakes were made. The schematic diagrams confused and seem to have fallen by the wayside as have the yellow cards for dyslexia and most examiners now use ways more suitable for the candidates.

There are those keen to learn about the difficulties who in a friendly way ask candidates about the effects of their conditions as they drive along. *"I am keen to know more because my friend's son has problems."* This is not a good idea because of possible emotional distraction!

Most of my referrals come following negative learning experiences so I ask, *"Why did you not tell your Instructor about your problem?"* The common answer is, *"They did not ask."* We must observe, ask and understand, but how do we find out the meaning to what we are observing and when the evidence is plain to see, do we actually understand the message being given and do we have the experience to deal with it?

Some of the indications of a muddled brain are so clear if only we can interpret them. One instructor cited that he suspected dyspraxia lay at the root of the difficulties a high achieving academic student was experiencing. Suspicions were reinforced when she stated her 'placement ran from October, September, August, July, June, May to April.' This was the final piece in the jig saw for him and even though he thought the diagnosis was blatantly obvious, the student was offended when he suggested she may have an underlying problem. It is sometimes even more difficult for high achievers to accept why they are struggling.

My advice is that it is not advisable to formally diagnose, because we do not know, but that does not mean we should not recognise the effects that we are observing and so teach and examine accordingly. We cannot presume we will be told about any condition, but if we are, then that is a bonus to help us act accordingly.

iii) **Identification Strategies**

It is essential that neither examiners nor instructors diagnose. That is not our job and we do not have the experience or the skills, nor do we know the background to understand the specific reasons why a condition has or has not been identified. The background could lie in the availability or provision of finances rather than that of need, or in a family refusal to accept a given diagnosis. Our task as instructors is to build a picture through relaxed chat which can often be achieved by asking a few strategic questions: Which school did you go to? What subjects are you studying? What sports do you play? What are your interests? Do you ride a bike?

When they know you are interested in them as people, rather than in what you are going to impart to them, then they will open up because they will trust you and you will get your answers and so be best able to teach them. If they are reserved and don't like chatting, then I just talk about life and what we are observing as we drive along and introduce leading topics and invariably they join in. Occasionally I have taught those with little voluntary speech, but that does not mean they cannot communicate.

We do not need a formal diagnosis, but just relevant observations to help us discover how best to teach each individual, although it does help if we find there has been one written so we know what to say on the test application to ensure they receive a fair chance of success. ADIs are in a unique and privileged position to closely observe their client's behaviour and possibly for the first time help them understand and come to terms with problems they may have struggled with for all their lives. Their future education can now begin under the positive guidance of the ADI and the understanding care of the Examiner and hopefully a system which will allow them to function to their best.

Instructors can have a huge impact on not only the individual, but indirectly on society in general. We are influential in changing the lives of some by halting their slide into unemployment and worthlessness by changing their attitude to driving. The biggest danger on the road is not lack of skill, but a poor attitude. If we fail in our task our clients can again be knocked down and condemned to the failure they have become used to. The power to change lives is the motivation for being an ADI.

iv) <u>**The Effects of Dyspraxia**</u> *on Learning to Drive*

<u>**Dyspraxia**</u> can result in wide-ranging characteristics and may be linked to a number of other conditions. The definition originates from **praxis** – practical, which coupled with **dys** – difficulty – is a brain processing disorder resulting in the poor organisation of the various stages involving thought, language and movement.

It can be a result of an accident or Stroke – <u>impairment,</u> but what we are considering here is <u>immaturity</u> -a physical developmental condition.

It may be determined before birth, with the term 'Clumsy Child Syndrome' previously being used to describe the characteristics. Similar difficulties can be observed following minimal brain damage which may then be classified as Mild Cerebral Palsy.

Awkward, uncoordinated movements and erratic thought processes are typical and it may be possible to recognise the condition by observing the gait of the candidate, although any diagnosis must be avoided as these jerky movements could be caused by many other unconnected conditions.

As many as 10% of the population will have learnt to function adequately with aspects of Dyspraxia, even though it may be undiagnosed or masked for other reasons. As it is not an illness but a physical dysfunction, they may explain it away by saying *"I am just clumsy"* and unless very severe, they will not have regarded it as a 'disability'.

The instructor will encounter those who know they have problems but don't understand what they are, those who don't realise they have problems and maybe a few who actually have a diagnosis. Their difficulty in planning and organising their thoughts may have seriously held back their schooling and the confusing structure of some of the theory questions can seriously affect their ability to pass the Theory Test.

Dyspraxia is also known as <u>**Developmental Coordination Disorder**</u> so they will have lived with the condition all their lives, but it may only be recognised as a problem when the complicated coordination and thought processes required for learning to drive are brought to the fore. Their self-esteem may have been severely affected as they have sought to make sense of an unrecognised and undiagnosed condition and have been bewildered by why they, as intelligent and capable people, cannot succeed. It may be more obvious if they have experienced delayed walking or speech development and required earlier help to clearly formulate words, but they may still question how this can have an effect on their learning to drive.

These notes are to help ADIs and Examiners to understand the feelings that candidates with dyspraxia may be experiencing and through a deeper understanding of their needs, we can all help to provide them with a positive test experience. As it is not an illness, but a neurological condition there is no cure, so the job of the instructor is to guide and assist in establishing the client's own coping skills in whatever unorthodox ways may be appropriate, rather than to impose a 'correct way,' and for the examiner to understand that the condition may make the candidate perform in a different way or manner. 'Hesitancy' for one person may be just taking necessary 'Care' for a person with dyspraxia and the reasons must be understood and catered for.

They have often perfected excuses to avoid sport and just accepted being unable to be neat and tidy or to remember sequences and patterns which may have affected their mathematical ability to remember their tables, (dysnumerate). In other educational areas such as the free creative aspects of English, Music and Art they may have excelled, but now, they have to come face to face with their suppressed demons. Not only do they not understand themselves, but they may find that their instructors also do not understand their thought processes or their actions, which just compounds their feeling of failure. To be effective, their learning must be in a **developmental creative style** rather than a directed formal one.

Some will have found sports activities involving eye/ hand/foot coordination problematic, whilst others may have struggled with fine writing control or the sequential processing involved in dressing and tying shoe laces and buttons, using a knife and fork, opening bottles and cans or experienced confusion when using a mirror and trying to convert and understand a mirror image and may at first struggle with smooth steering. Rhythm will be difficult and they are unlikely to have been naturally able to ride a bike, which is not really surprising if we consider the two sides of the brain struggling to work together with all the multi-tasking required.

I am sure there will be those who can't see how these clients can or should drive safely, but all I can say is that they may be different to teach, but once they have learnt, with the new patterns being firmly established they can function as safely as other drivers. As with all disabilities there may be the rare occasions where one cannot drive because their problems are too severe, but if they have been given the chance, they can accept this because they have been provided with the 'opportunity' and not told they cannot before they have tried. Each stage has to be taught and reinforced separately as they may find the transferral of skills learnt in one situation quite difficult to apply to another. **'We did that last week'** may not mean that they can do it this week, even though it is in a related situation.

One highly literate woman explained that she viewed herself as a marionette where all her limbs functioned, but they all acted on their own and it was difficult to coordinate any movement together. Trying to do two things at once was impossible, so walking and carrying anything upstairs had to be avoided. The two sides of the brain may not be fluently linked, so activities involving both hemispheres such as the T in R sequences can be difficult to process and each driving stage needs to be isolated, so 'dry-steering' may be the only way to achieve this successfully. They have to learn one thing at a time. One asked in amazement *"you expect me to use two hands and two feet together?"* A manual car can be very demanding!

They may have been 'mistakenly' classed as dyslexic because the poor coordination of the brain function can have caused problems with maths, reading, spelling and formal writing and they may cover up by blaming their 'stupidity' or their 'inability' to drive, instead of realising they have a different, but recognised condition. If they understood the effects more, it would enable them to devise their own coping strategies.

Instructors and examiners have to be able to recognise and understand why the candidate may be experiencing difficulties and to be aware they must not compound the problem by unnecessary requests or distractions. The instructor also must exercise extreme tact in addressing what is observed and in seeking background information, as it can be a very sensitive area to explore since frustration, anger, flash-backs and depression may be lurking just beneath the surface.

I begin my research of their learning needs by asking about cycling, sport or art and the subjects they have selected to study. It is unlikely they will have chosen to progress with mathematics or even classical music where sequences and fine patterns are involved and they are unlikely to have been successful at the sports involving the quick coordination necessary for catching, throwing, kicking or balancing or with activities such as fine drawing or cutting with scissors. They may though be good at games such as snooker where time is available for the planning required or be quite artistic when relating to colour, texture, design and shapes and may informally play a musical instrument where they can be creative.

As with all spectrums there will be many variations and the vast majority will not have had any formal diagnosis or classification attached to their condition since, most likely, it will have been viewed as a problem they would grow out of, or they will have subconsciously learnt daily coping and avoidance strategies. It may only manifest itself in a serious form when learning to drive or **under the stress of a test**, so for most sufferers a formal declared history is unlikely to be available.

It is impossible to generalise, but those with the condition may cope by 'going into themselves', often becoming isolated or depressed, with males directing their intellectual skills in one specific area of interest or becoming frustrated and angry, whilst females may be overtly verbose about their stupidity and clumsiness or mask and excuse the problem by being 'dippy'. The most difficult job of the instructor is to be able to identify the hidden indications of such conditions and to be able to relate to and address the evidence without causing further stress. Their frustration may lead to a tendency to opt out of things that are too difficult, so don't be surprised if they give up or get frustrated or even stroppy, and try to be sensitive to understand the reasons why. Being misjudged is soul destroying and is what often happens to those with **Hidden Difficulties.**

The examiner has even less time to make his assessment, but as they walk to the car he may get a clue by observing if the candidate moves in a jaunty manner or plodding ('walking in treacle') or if they accentuate their movements in the form of a skip. The run, skip or spring is used as a coping strategy to enable the jerky movement to become smoother.

They may find it difficult to turn and change direction or struggle to use the key or open the bonnet or may be clumsy as they get into the car. It is more likely they will use an automatic car since they may have struggled with the processing required for manual driving and it is easier than having to admit they have a condition which sets them apart from their peers.

The medical background of the condition is not usually relevant to driving, but dyspraxia is thought to be caused by an immature development of the neurones of the brain which transport information to the limbs, but even here there are differences of medical opinion and it is not in the brief of driving professionals to understand the causes. But an understanding of the effects is necessary and if the specific 'information- pathway' is in any way compromised, then the resulting movements may become jerky or the initial stimulation may find another route or passage which results in delayed action. In extreme circumstances of stress the direction may short circuit which could result in extreme manifestations of panic and if not controlled could, in a driving context, be dangerous. An intention to turn right may be compromised by the message going in the wrong direction resulting in turning left with a right indicator showing.

If the candidate has not already selected their preference for ID, then this is when the examiner must ask which method of ID they would prefer to use, since for most with dyspraxia, the sequential memory or the use of schematic diagrams could trigger panic and failure. It is to be avoided just like the warning on television for epilepsy sufferers that flashing lights will be on the news report. It is obvious that Schematic Diagrams must be a no-go area and if dyspraxia has not been declared, then in the interests of Road Safety the examiner must be able to understand that if they give sequential memory requests it could trigger confusion and any sudden change of direction to get them 'back on course' could be dangerous.

The avoidance of stress is essential and unnecessary practice or the focusing on an error, can stimulate even more failure, which can then become ingrained. I have taught those who under stress have become muddled by intrusive instructions which has resulted in uncontrolled and 'violent' movements of the steering wheel or gear lever. Over time this 'spasticity' has become less and less until it has no longer been an issue and they have been able to drive smoothly. The formal use of Q&A must be avoided as it is likely to cause a wipe-out of the mind and anyway, the skilled instructor is able to **assess the level of learning by observing,** without the need for intrusive questioning. The application of knowledge is important, not the verbalisation or skill to be able to answer questions.

An important aim of the instructor is to teach coping skills to help the client avoid unnecessary stress, but we must always be aware that test-stress could cause regression, which would not usually be manifest in their independent driving, so examiners also need to understand the issues so they can avoid creating increased stress through unclear requests.

Candidates are sometimes failed because the examiner has misunderstood the motive behind the actions, rather than them having actually made an error which has resulted in any serious consequences and at times the error is directly as a result of the examiner's late instructions. It must always be remembered that it is the candidate's test and not the examiner's and candidates must be encouraged to drive using their own developed skills and coping strategies, which they have learnt to enable them to become comfortably safe drivers. The examiner is there to observe a safe drive and candidates must not be seen as being necessarily wrong if they drive independently as they would when driving on their own, rather than acting under the examiner's specific requirements.

Examples of this would be that if the mirror image confuses or overwhelms the brain, then its pedantic use could in certain situations be dangerous, but the use of general peripheral vision could achieve the same safe results and could in fact be the candidate's developed safe personal strategy; or in order to process a manoeuvre, there may be a delay as they struggle to organise the sequence in the correct order and so a gear change may be made earlier to enable their processing to have time to negotiate the junction safely. It may not be the ideal eco driving style, or what the examiner would do when he drove, but the question to be posed is whether it is actually wrong or dangerous.

It is therefore vital that instructions are given clearly and in good time with the message reinforced through pointing, as they will find it difficult to remember more than one instruction at a time. The candidate should therefore not be marked down for making errors for a late gear change or for missing a mirror if the instruction has been given too late for them. It takes extra time for them to process the examiner's verbal instructions and in the time available, convert them into the required physical processes when acting under instructions, which is of course an alien intrusion into their normal independent safe driving process.

To avoid the strategies used being misinterpreted, it would help if we could all perceive these candidates as having a physical disability with which they are struggling to cope. It would then be easier to accept their 'misdemeanours', but life has never been easy for them because they appear to be 'normal,' and their actions can be misjudged by strangers, especially under test-stress. Some of the best instructors and examiners for Specific Needs are those who have experienced difficulties themselves.

I taught a dyspraxic woman with only a right arm, who still got confused with which way to turn since it was the brain-processing which was confused and not the physical process. Her intention was correct, but the muddle between the brain and the limb can be very distressing to the person concerned as they know what they intended to do, but the opposite action is the result. It is therefore important for them to learn how to manage the condition and its effects on their driving.

As in this example the visible physical effects were easy to overcome, but the hidden thought processing can be very problematic especially on test, since it is not always clear how the information given to them will be processed and subsequently expressed. It can make them feel very embarrassed when their actions are contra to what they may have intended them to be, especially when in front of a stranger in a position of authority. My explanation of the process is what we used to call going 'haywire' (or wire-wool) which is very difficult to unravel and one is not quite sure where the end will come out.

A lifetime of coping strategies can become ravelled under the stress of a driving test, as happened when one of my candidates decided to negotiate a roundabout anticlockwise, or when another tried to follow an arrow pointing the opposite way. Many Examiners and ADIs will have experienced those who have switched the right indicator and then turned left or got confused with what to do when they saw both 30 and 40 written on the carriageway-(one upside down.) The confusion would not normally happen, because they would drive within their comfort zone and avoid stressful test situations.

The haze of the test can also cause the operation of switches and handbrakes to become greatly confused as the levers are pushed and pressed in all directions in an attempt to hopefully switch them on or release them. The positions up, down, backwards, or forwards are difficult words to interpret and in the early stages of learning they may lose position of the gear lever or gears and have to look at them. A test used to assess the balance of the brain following stroke is to see if they can point to the end of their nose with both hands with their eyes closed. Switches may become trial and error, so cars with fiddly multi-position switching systems should be avoided for such clients. A client's difficulty may not indicate an inability or a lack of experience, since they may be fine when using a less complicated system and may be able to overcome their problems when driving a suitable automatic car which gives them more time to think with fewer switches and levers to process. This can then enable them to establish a clear pathway within the brain.

It may help our understanding of their difficulties if we consider the massive amount of brain power required to negotiate a roundabout even for the 'normal' driver and if we test ourselves by approaching one whilst verbally breaking down and talking through all the processes required, it is revealing just how much distance has been covered in such a short time and how distracted we can become by the exercise.

The enormity of the problem is even clearer if we then think of the driver acting under alien instruction and stress and add on the extra time involved for the brain processing of the dyspraxic driver to listen to the instruction, register it, process and translate the meaning, before being able to select the appropriate pathway in the brain available for the action to take. Then compare this with the simple action of going down the known, pre-prepared route they would use on their daily independent commute.

If we add into this scenario the dyspraxic candidate with English as a Second or Foreign Language then the problems become even clearer. 'Turn Left' has to be translated into their own language, transposed into the appropriate direction, before being converted into the required action, so it becomes clear how important the timing and clarity of the examiner's instructions are to the success of the client with dyspraxia.

A poor short term memory can have surprising consequences and ADIs often talk about learners forgetting or day dreaming. I was giving directions to one lad as he approached a 'Give Way,' where he stopped unnecessarily and waited. I asked why he had stopped when the road was clear. He explained, *"If I press the clutch it wipes my mind of which way is right and which is left, so I have to stop and think."* This could be interpreted as 'losing concentration' as they struggle to synchronise the brain cogs, but in fact they are concentrating extra hard and not being lazy.

Examiners must also be careful not to distract candidates by leading them off into pathways of conversation as they may not be able to switch back easily and quickly when required and under their own decision making process they would have chosen not to talk, but they answer because they believe that under exam conditions it may be deemed to be rude not to. They can appear to be listening, but the result is not what the instructor expects because they may hear an 'abridged' version which is actually different to what the instructor believes he has said.

Some of us have witnessed the brains of our clients shut down when on tests and they have been faced with remembering a nine point sequence from a schematic diagram, but if we consider that they have no map reading ability, little sense of direction, have difficulty in distinguishing right from left and struggle to remember any sequence more than one, it is hardly surprising. I observed one examiner struggle to keep control when my candidate's mind 'crashed' on the seventh part of the sequence, but with sitting in the back, I had seen the wipe-out developing and would have aborted the requirement before the emergency arose.

The main aspect of teaching these students is where possible to avoid, but also to teach how to cope with cognitive stress. The brain is an unbelievably complex organ which we are only just beginning to understand, so we have to train them to switch off from cognitive distraction or they may 'lose it' when overwhelmed.

I have not covered ADHD in this book, but the condition can be associated with dyspraxia – difficulty in flexible thinking, a poor attention span, easily distracted and reacting to sensory stimulation without having the natural automatic controls. A horn can trigger a jerky response, rather like the startle reflex spasm one might see from someone with Cerebral Palsy. They may be unable to sense the direction of an emergency vehicle and be only capable of doing one thing at a time properly, but they may still try to do many things at once. Overload can cause them to become unfocused and erratic, leading to poor concentration and a 'messy' performance, which may result in emotional outbursts and low self-esteem.

If ADIs are concerned as to whether the learner is coping, then change the activity or reduce the load because they have a tendency to be erratic and have 'good and bad days.' Teach them to do things in stages so they are never overwhelmed. As soon as they begin to struggle, then move on because they don't learn if they are stressed. Increased cognition load can result in overload and you may not know what is on their mind to distract. I have sometimes spent part of a lesson discussing the personal problems of a client and afterwards questioned myself as to whether that was my role, but when I see them come bouncing out and eager for the next lesson because the load has been lifted and we can then put in a full session of hard graft, I realise that the learning only took place because we had resolved the problem and reached a stage where learning was possible.

The easiest way I explain the condition to myself is to say my computer has dyspraxic tendencies. Most of the time it works well; sometimes it is smart and slick, then at other times I can hear it crackling under the load and I don't understand why. My solution is shut it down and switch it off. A few minutes later and it will be smart and on the ball again. Personally I cat nap for a few minutes and then I can also be back functioning well again, but if I don't switch off, I cannot work effectively, any more than my computer can.

Our customer's brains are just computers and we have to be able to understand them and occasionally be prepared to switch them off, rather than overwork them. If your struggling learner shows a few of these symptoms then maybe they require more appropriate or different methods to teach them to drive independently. Dyspraxia may be at the root of their confusion.

v) **The Effects of Dyslexia** *on Learning to Drive*

Except for those who struggle with the Theory Test, few people with Dyslexia are actually prevented from driving because of their dyslexia. There are many famous dyslexic drivers who have attained professional success through their driving (Jackie Stewart) or in other activities such as dancing (Kara Tointon) where precise movement is required. I have also taught pupils in school with extremely severe dyslexia who have not experienced any problems when learning to drive.

As Dyslexia became an 'acceptable' condition I found that people with other hidden conditions such as Dyspraxia used the term to get the help which would otherwise not be available to them. It does not really matter what the root is or term we use, but we need to be aware that Hidden Difficulties are very real and that instructors and examiners need to provide a different environment to enable these students to flourish and that the Specific Needs covered in this book are very real. One young man said he 'avoided' his previous instructor who lived locally, because he was embarrassed at not being able to 'learn' from him. I wonder if the instructor was embarrassed at not being able to 'teach' him?

The cross-over between the various terminologies used to describe similar conditions is irrelevant and in many cases has hindered the provision available especially if the specific charities are precious of the stated condition for which they advocate. Over the years this division has allowed government agencies to ignore the issues or to only latch on to what is cheap to provide.

Instead of looking at the whole issue of Specific Needs and providing what is required, the DVSA have tried to 'divide and rule' by negotiating with only one specific agency at a time. At one time it was Dyslexia and then Autism, but it seems unable to appreciate the depths of the common problems which may affect **all** those with a variety of hidden difficulties. This results in only one small armchair perspective of the issues being considered, instead of really researching the effects of all these conditions when driving at speed, in control of a moving car, under the stress of instruction and test. When the concerns discussed were ignored, the credibility of all involved was undermined.

In many cases Dyslexia is a misnomer and therefore it is a misleading title which often results in the actual condition being dismissed because the student is able to read. This causes the student to feel at a loss because they cannot find a tag for their condition, or receive the help they require, so when they start to drive they may become defensive if the instructor seeks to discover if there is any dyslexia in the family.

Much scientific research into brain function is now taking place and dyslexia is thought to be caused by different brain patterning and therefore the need to process information in different areas of the brain outside of the norm. This causes them to interpret stimuli in uncoordinated patterns. It is certainly not a disability because the ability to see life differently can stimulate incredible creativity, so it should not necessarily be deemed as a negative, but it should be recognised as **a condition** with support strategies being developed to assist functioning and to prevent society viewing it as a 'disability,' instead of being able to see and appreciate the different skills.

There are estimated to be six million dyslexic people in Britain; 10% of the population with 4% having severe symptoms.

A difficulty in Reading is not necessarily caused by Dyslexia as they may have other conditions or may have been inappropriately taught. Not all non-readers are dyslexic, although it is often used as a convenient term.

Fluency in Reading does not necessarily preclude dyslexia as some people with dyslexic tendencies can read fluently because they are able to use other strengths of context and language to develop their reading skills.

What has dyslexia got to do with driving? Many people have little understanding of how it could affect their learning, so if they struggle, they don't attribute it to their dyslexia or explain their difficulty to their instructor as they do not see it as relevant to learning a practical skill.

The spectrum is very broad. Severe dyslexics may find they don't have problems, whilst others with only minor tendencies may have serious difficulties. They may have presumed that because they have learnt coping strategies within the classroom, then it will not affect their driving, but of course in a speeding vehicle, they haven't the time to use their learnt strategies because they have to take time to evaluate the situation and engage the system and it is often then too late.

The Primary effect may be a delay in processing. If the brain stimuli have to take a muddled pathway then it will take more time, so this delay is what affects drivers the most. The strategies they have developed become irrelevant in this new and dangerous environment and this causes stress, which at times can become very severe and manifest in a variety of ways. They must be helped to develop their planning skills to give them more time to decide and act safely and prevent being overwhelmed.

An Initial solution to find the time required can be obtained by first using an automatic car. This leaves time for the brain processing to kick in and to process what is happening. Owing to external pressures there may be a certain reticence so they need to be helped to analyse their condition to enable them to understand that it is not their difficulty in using the clutch or gears which has triggered this advice, but the need to smoothly process what is happening on the road. Once the reason is understood it is invariably accepted and they can always learn manual when they have developed natural driving skills and the stress has gone. Examiners and Instructors need to be aware that, although it is not always the case, those who present for test in Automatic cars may have additional undeclared difficulties and a dyslexic tendency may be at the root of their choice.

The Secondary effects of a muddled mind can be confusion with the concept of right and left which takes time to sort out. In real life driving, careful planning using the Sat Navs arrows can help, but trying to puzzle out and interpret the verbal instructions of another can be quite problematic. Terms such as Nearside or Offside or Left and Right should be avoided unless accompanied by pointing, but 'My side' and 'Your Side' are terms which are usually understood and some feel happier to write left and right on their hand or wear a ring to identify a particular hand. This is very personal and the methods they have previously employed may be inappropriate. Children may have been taught to use the 'L' pattern formed by their left index finger and thumb, but the time taken to look would be inappropriate when driving. Precise pointing by the instructor is normally required and is the process which should be followed by the examiner.

Reading signs. Essentially one learns to read by using a mixture of phonics, word recognition and contextual clues. Recognising and interpreting road destinations first requires the specific skills of **scanning** to select the relevant sign, followed by the identification of the shapes, letters and words from a mass of other information; translating it into a verbal word and interpreting it into a destination, then direction and the MSPSGL routine.

If we consider how difficult this is for the 'normal' reader, it becomes obvious how complex and time consuming it is for the dyslexic brain to find the relevant pathways. Selecting the correct lane is further complicated when the brain with a right - left confusion gets muddled by similar shapes, colours and word patterns. There is so much information-overload on approach to junctions which is then further complicated by the need to scan, select and download from different coloured signs whilst travelling at speed. It would help on test if Primary destination signs were chosen, rather than being rushed to read Secondary signs with black print on a white background just before entry to the junction. -*"My reading isn't that bad, but with the added complexity of driving at the same time it breaks down. I end up going around roundabouts several times, scanning for my destination sign."*

Some find that within a study context, the number of words on the page may become jumpy and muddled if printed on a stark white background, so they may choose to provide a specifically coloured lens to reduce the contrast. Although this is not relevant to most, some may be more comfortable using tinted glasses when reading and driving, which could be particularly relevant for instructors when helping with the theory.

As with any eye condition, what helps one will be a hindrance to another, so rather than instructors selecting for them what they use, they may choose to provide their own personalised coloured transparency to cover the words. Sunglasses are often required to help them when driving and in the same way choose which colour suits for the number plate test.

What effects do instructors encounter? I have had students totally panic at the thought of reading the words on signs, yet who seem to be able to read from a static page reasonably well. There are many reasons for this, but primarily they are flashbacks to school and the feeling of being stupid and the fear of being asked to read from the blackboard. One of the indicators used in the identification of dyslexia is those students who cannot take notes from the blackboard and feel imprisoned by the wall of words.

They may be able to read, they may be able to write, they may even be able to spell, but the effort of the memory involved to transfer the information from one medium to another becomes problematic. This is why some dyslexic readers find they have difficulty reading similar shaped destinations on road signs when they have to look and read and then interpret the meaning and put it into action without having any **contextual clues** to make sense of it. They may have the same shape and same beginning and end with a similar medial pattern, but without any use of context they are indistinguishable and will confuse or delay the processing.

These candidates would probably say they were able to read adequately because they would use contextual clues to 'cloze' the information being received. They may not even be regarded as having a Specific Need, because of the coping strategies they had developed over many years, but they would still struggle with these words out of context. **There is more to reading than barking at print** and the cognition involved whilst on the move, does not really kick in immediately since the brain power is being used for the process of the driving and recognising the sign, rather than comprehending the semantics of the information on it

When undertaking Independent Driving, those dyslexics with a reasonable sequential memory could choose the Schematic Diagrams as the lesser of two evils, but they may then be confused by the diagrams because of the lack of scale, context, orientation and the number of shapes that would just overwhelm them. I know some would regard it as 'teaching for test,' but as part of test preparation the ADI may need to give reading lessons of the **specific signs and the place names** they may encounter and practise the routes they may use.

For those with both reading and sequential memory confusion then training needs to be undertaken in using memory cards. For my own personal use I slot cards into my Sat-Nav holder on the dash board. I can then clearly see the route. I use arrows and numbers with circles as the best abbreviations because they don't need translating from R and L. It helps to state significant places; 'Station, Pub, Church or Supermarket.' It is vital to add scale and distance between junctions.

After the problems the schematic diagrams caused, most examiners now use a mixture of methods to suit the needs of the candidate.

When struggling with word recognition, it is vital that precise wording is used. Take the direction which says **All Routes** is quite different to the one which says **All Other Routes**. To the dyslexic, the double check required can involve travelling quite a few extra metres and they may then find they are too near the junction. Anyone doubting the level of these difficulties has only to drive in a foreign country to appreciate the navigational problems of scanning and reading jumbled letters or shapes. In real life these drivers would plan and learn their routes and make their own notes and just as the Word Processor has been the lifeline which has rescued many dyslexic Students, so have Sat-Navs been the lifeline for many dyslexic Drivers.

The clarity of verbal instructions would benefit from being reinforced by pointing, since what may seem to be a clear direction can be misinterpreted. *"I would like you to take the next turning left which is at the top of the hill."* This would seem to be very clear, yet what is remembered is *"at the top of the hill"* and the turn left is forgotten, so when they reach the top of the hill and start to look for the left turn and then decide which direction is left, they have already driven past. It is quite revealing to ask what they thought the instruction was and it is even more important for the examiners to make their instructions perfectly clear and point to reinforce.

We cannot underestimate the psychological stress dyslexic students have been under for most of their lives. They try very hard to listen, but because it does not always make immediate sense or they do not respond immediately, the comments they are conditioned to hear are, *"You are not concentrating,"* or "*Listen to what I am saying,"* or "*You would have known, if you had listened."* "*Pay attention."* Even if these words are not used by ADIs, the same attitude can often be unintentionally transmitted and received. Their coping strategies must be understood, rather than criticised or regarded as a fault. They may wait a lot longer before acting because the processing takes longer to compute, but that should not be regarded as hesitation, but taking care.

Many times I have to hold back from saying *"Hurry up,"* and have to remind myself that it does not matter if they are not as quick as I may be as long as they are driving safely and rather than the instructor impulsively jumping in and taking action, they may need to carefully consider how much more time is needed to plan for situations. Teaching early action is particularly necessary since if Examiners apply the duals, the candidates invariably say they were already taking action. It is therefore important to be taught how to avoid panicking the examiner into unnecessary braking.

Dyslexia is a neurological condition and not laziness, so we cannot expect them to do things in the same way as others. If they are disorganised or lose the study sheets we give them, it does not indicate laziness or a lack of care. In fact they may have tried extremely hard and feel embarrassed by their lack of memory. Low self-esteem may appear as lacking motivation, but we need to look beneath to see the real cause. That does not excuse the few who may play on their difficulties and sometimes a sharp retort is required, but for others a different solution can be found.

I taught one youth who could not follow the analogue speedometer. Being unable to tell the time on an analogue dial is quite common amongst dyslexics, so I overcame the problem by fitting a satellite digital speedometer. I could easily have presumed he was deliberately not keeping to the speed, rather than asking and finding that it was because he could not understand the analogue system. They need to be taught the composition of a number plate since once they understand it they find it easier to read, but if it causes serious problems, then provide a felt tip and pad or pointing grid so they can draw it for the examiner. These solutions are no different to the additions we use to help those with physical difficulties; extra mirrors, steering spinners or quick release handbrakes.

Just as I can never remember people's names, it can be impossible for those with dyslexia to remember addresses or road names. *"Can you drop me off at my grandmother's?" "Where does she live?" "I will know when I get there!!"* We drove around until he recognised a shop and then he was able to recognise the road because driving is about doing and not about listening or remembering or following abstract directions. I have taught those who struggle to do any fine work (switches) and yet their gross motor skills are good and also taught those whose gross motor skills are poor and yet can knit and sew. There are no set rules as to how the learners may be affected.

Always look 'beneath' and the 'hidden' will soon become clear.

vi) **An ADI's view of being Dyslexic**

Probably the biggest surprise I received after writing my first book were those ADIs who contacted me to thank me saying that not only had it changed their approach to their teaching, but it had also helped them to understand themselves and to realise that the problems they had struggled with all their lives may have had their roots in dyslexia. I did begin to wonder if this was the normal percentage of dyslexics in society or whether people with dyslexia were attracted to being driving instructors!

In order to help other instructors understand the problem more deeply, an ADI wrote the following. I include it here as it gives us a succinct explanation from one of our own, to which many of us will be able to relate.

"I thought I would give some understanding into Dyslexia from what it is like to live with it. I love reading and am a fast reader and like big print books so I can clearly see every word. I don't understand nouns or verbs and took forever to understand vowels. I get letters mixed up b/d and z/s. I don't know my left from my right and had to practice which was my ring finger by putting a bracelet on my right hand so I knew the other one was the correct one. On lessons I just point and say" that way".

I won't talk to anyone I don't know, as when I am nervous I stutter and can say a random wrong word and feel stupid. I have no sense of direction, but once I have been to a place I can remember where to go. I can't remember street names or names and I don't know the streets around where I live. I have to think very carefully before I speak to make sure the right words come out.

My handwriting is awful and I am so happy that Word Processing exists and Spell Checking. I spell phonetically and it took me years to understand that Knife is spelled with a K and not a C. I have no grammar and don't understand it. I have no short term memory so the ID part of the test would fill me with panic. I have spent my life being told I was thick. I can't do maths and don't understand anything above adding. Everything takes time to understand. When I am going to a new place I spend time looking at the words of the places I will be going through so I can recognise them on the signs. Motorways are easy as I just have to know the number which I come off at. I hold maps in the way I am going.

I hope this has given everyone a bit of an insight into the ways Dyslexia can affect you. It affects everyone differently. Some are like me and quite severe, whilst others just get the odd letter mixed up."

vii) **The Effects of Autistic Spectrum Condition** *on Learning to Drive*

ASC/ASD covers a wide spectrum of characteristics which, (although a separate condition,) may be linked to dyspraxia. Many people who would appear to function quite normally have aspects of the 3 main classifications. It is not an illness, but an individual personality difference.

Autism: severe cases will not be able to relate to other road users well enough to enable them to drive safely. Those who do may appear to be extremely shy or even refuse to speak, (elective mutes) make odd sounds and only feel complete within their own world. The car environment allows them to be relaxed and become competent drivers and can enable them to function normally, comfortably and safely within their own metal box.

Aspergers: often highly intelligent, avid researchers, incredibly knowledgeable within a specific narrow field of interest, but may lack understanding of what would normally be recognised as basic life matters. They can switch from adult to childlike behaviour and become stressed by the unfamiliar. They may be very verbose and appear to be superior, but can be **extremely anxious** and detached from reality and will be happier in adult 'sensible' company. As they see life differently they enrich our lives with 'humour' and use of language and if guided correctly, they can learn to drive

Semantic Pragmatic Disorder: a difficulty in understanding language in normal usage. They can experience severe problems with complex Theory Questions and will require detailed explanations with which they may argue, because to their way of thinking, the answer is illogical. The knowledge will be there, but the required answer may not be forthcoming, although a rational explanation may be expressed. They may however not understand why their 'correct' answer is unacceptable.

Having developed Social Skills they may present as 'normal', but Q&A is often irrelevant and may cause panic or mental freezing as they try to work out what the question means and what response is required. They find it difficult to fully understand through the medium of speech and may take words literally without the ability to accept subtle hints or any understanding of innuendo. If language is clear and direct they can function very competently in practical activities such as driving.

Test candidates are unlikely to be prepared to state their condition on their application as it is personal to who they are as people and they would not see themselves as being abnormal or disabled. In fact they would perceive the other people to be different for not being able or prepared to accept their particular characteristics. This may have led to bullying, withdrawal and self harm. They can behave in fixed and formulated patterns as there is a right and wrong way to behave, so if others are in the wrong, then they are the ones who should make the necessary changes and rather than be impetuous, they will wait until the situation is resolved. It is often black and white. Examples on test-

-A candidate turning right at a roundabout found his exit lane partially blocked on both the right and left, but leaving a gap in the middle. He waited for one car blocking his way to reverse to allow his free passage. The reason for this extra care was not appreciated by the examiner so he failed for positioning.

-Another candidate was about to begin to reverse round the corner when a car approached so he correctly waited. The driver turned into his drive, got out, opened the boot, collected his belongings, opened the door of the house, walked in and closed the door. The candidate knew he could now continue as the danger was over. He passed with a hesitation d/f as the examiner said, "I realised he was a bit different".

Face to face discussion is difficult, but they are also unlikely to be able to converse by phone, since the social clues are absent. The suggested phone call from the DVSA seeking information would be inappropriate for them and bizarre or amusing conversations can often develop on lessons. In an attempt to break the ice at the start of a test one examiner asked,

"What shall I call you?" *Call me what you like.*
"What do you friends call you?" *I don't have any friends.*
"What does your mother call you?" *It depends -----*

As they walked to the car a somewhat inappropriate question was asked, *"Oh you have Aspergers. How does that affect you?"*

Well Aspergers is a broad spectrum condition, so it would take a long time to explain the number of effects it has on me.

During the test,

"Well it is not as bad as you expected is it?

You have not given me the result yet!!

The initial conversation can often be the indicator for the examiner to realise he will require empathetic understanding to conduct the test in an appropriate way. Candidates are unlikely to make normal eye contact, often looking down at the floor, but on the other hand may scrutinise the examiner's face as they attempt to comprehend and relate. In order to adequately test their driving ability, the examiner will need to avoid distraction and give clear precise instructions reinforced by pointing.

A choice of ID must be offered as for many the Sequential Memory Test has proved to be actually dangerous owing to the brain being overwhelmed by the task of memory, rather than it being fully available to be used for safe driving. On tests I have observed both total panic and those where the switch to concentrate on the traffic has wiped the mind of the required sequence. This resulted in the candidate's embarrassment as the examiner was required to take a detour to get back on track.

They find the schematic diagrams a distraction, and believe it safer to try to remember the sequence rather than look and be distracted. They have to be in total control of their driving, so if they do not see the purpose of something or it disturbs their concentration, they will have learnt to use avoidance strategies to cope with the distraction. This is a major part of teaching them to drive safely where they learn to prioritise and switch, so it is an anachronism for them then to be tested on their short term sequential memory recall under the stress of test.

An interesting aspect is that when a pattern is fully established, it will then become permanent and they will remember the route in great pedantic detail, (even commenting on what the person at the traffic lights was wearing or the breed of dogs) In a known location and with practice they will be able to follow a route completely accurately or when following Sat Nav instructions, so truly independent driving will not cause them any problems. Reading is not usually difficult and they may be able to learn rote facts such as Railway Timetables or detailed road routes and destinations, but their difficulty lies in their relationship with the verbal instruction and the need to interpret its meaning so as to remember in the short term. This may be an impossible hurdle to overcome and why they require to be given the destination signs and numbers to read when on test.

I asked an examiner why he had chosen to give a 9 part (4+3+2) Sequential Memory Test to a highly intelligent candidate with declared Aspergers and was taken aback by the reply *"I did not think he would be able to read the destination signs as Aspergers is like Dyslexia."* This comment triggered these guidelines as I realised that examiners are doing their best, but they are uninformed and the DVSA emphasis on **Dyslexia** has in some cases blinkered their minds to the other Hidden Disabilities.

When concern for these candidates is raised, the official response is 'they are able to ask the examiner for reinforcement', but asking help from a stranger is not something they would ever do in real life, so to ask an official test examiner in a position of power to repeat the instructions would be too stressful or even impossible. There are those who would be more able to write a letter than ask a face to face question. To query an examiner would be beyond their communication and emotional skills.

In theory, provision has been made for these disorders, but in practice it is not always complied with and the struggle for these candidates to remember the sequences has proved to be both torturous and dangerous. *'this could be by asking you which method you prefer - following traffic signs or a series of directions (a maximum of three), which are supported by a diagram. In some cases this may be shortened to just two directions.* (DVSA guidelines)

Their difficulty in performing this part of the test does not of course imply they are not perfectly capable drivers, but that it is inappropriate to test them by using these methods. They may happily use technology, since those with these difficulties usually relate to inanimate objects more easily than to people, or they may use Post-it notes, not only to trigger their memory, but also to prevent the memory from being overwhelmed by the task of attempting to remember, when the traffic conditions require their full concentration. I am sure I am not the only ADI who uses a Sat Nav and Post-it notes and know that I would struggle on a test to remember and recall three sequences of instructions whilst coping with the changing traffic conditions.

By nature they are inflexible, so in order to learn to drive safely they must be exposed to how to cope with situations which are constantly changing. The direct retort *"You said!"* should not be taken as an aggressive response, but a desire to comprehend that what you said in one context is now different, because the situation has changed. They may appear to be rude, but *"Got it! Got it!"* means they now understand. If the instructor repeats something they already know, or uses 'mirror' as a one word prompt, they may receive an aggressive *"I know! I know!"* What the instructor means is 'you are not doing it correctly,' but 'shorthand/shortspeech' is difficult for them to interpret and it may receive a hasty retort which must not be interpreted as a refusal to listen or learn.

There are not many things a person with Aspergers cannot achieve, but there are those with Semantic Pragmatic Disorder who have been prevented from passing the Theory Test because of the DVSA's insistence on it being a memory-based test rather than knowledge-based. Exasperated parents often say, *"When I rephrase the question, he knows the answer."* The refusal to allow candidates to ask their readers for explanations of the more complex questions, (as they would be able to in education exams) discriminates against them because of their disability. They usually score highly on the HPT and it is not through lack of practical ability that they are prevented from driving, because as long as they are understood and taught in a different way, they can learn to drive safely. If the testing is done according to their strengths and their learnt strategies, rather than facing them with what they cannot do, then they can legally become integrated into the driving community.

The smartly dressed young man with the social skills who presents for test may mask these ASC characteristics which the examiners now need to be experienced enough to identify. Otherwise they may continue to make the wrong judgements which have become more obvious since the introduction of ID and desire of instructors to sit in and observe tests.

ASC covers a wide spectrum of the most interesting and creative people who have much to contribute to our society and must be recognised as valuable in their own right with an equal opportunity to attain a licence through 'differentiation'. Their interpretation and understanding of life is just as acceptable as the formulated bureaucratic one that the Civil Servants expect them to pedantically follow, but this concept seems difficult for both sides to comprehend. The DVSA believe that as they are not an Educational establishment, but a Standards one, they don't have to comply with Access.

viii) **How can we teach those with Hidden Difficulties?**

Some comments from instructors about those with Hidden Difficulties are: "they don't remember what I tell them"; "they ignore simple instructions"; "what they can do one day they have forgotten by the next"; and *"they do exactly the opposite from what I tell them."* On the other hand the complaint made by their learners is: *"he keeps telling me things and expecting me to listen and understand, but I don't learn like that."* The problem lies in them being **'asked to do'**, rather than being **'allowed to do'** what comes naturally to them, even if it is different from what the Instructor expects them to do.

Is it a difficult learner or the instructor having difficulty?

The ADIs often believe they have to teach instead of facilitating students to learn in whatever way is best for them and examiners believe they have to examine rather than provide opportunities for candidates to drive to the best of their ability. I term this **Developmental Driving** -when learners develop their own style of comfortable safe driving under the instructor's guidance, rather than listening to what he wants them to do and the examiner allowing them to show what they can do, rather than expecting them to do what they cannot, or don't actually need to do.

It is true that we cannot 'teach' some clients, but that does not mean they cannot learn and we can help them to learn by exposing them to as many hazards and diverse situations as possible so that they learn **experientially**. We can guide them to develop what they already have established through the many experiences they have had before they come to us and develop those skills through informal repetition. They learn through the drip, drip of experience and can succeed to drive independently in their own way, but honed by the instructor. It may be impossible to predict how they will perform the test, but it will be possible to say they will be safe considerate drivers. They don't need any questions or analysis or words. It is development through routine and this is how they live their lives; to the same shops and to the same workplace. They don't require the complexities we try to feed them or what we demand from them. Familiarisation and a comfortable environment desensitises them from any panic.

We need to recognise that in rural areas where there are no buses, learning to drive is an important factor in halting the vicious cycle of unemployment.

The instructor cannot aim for a set level of skill-perfection because they will probably not achieve it, but the learners will reach a satisfactory level where they will be able to drive safely and defensively. If they are set a standard they will not be able to reach, they will fail in despair, but if they are allowed to **develop,** they will become independently safe competent drivers. If they are expected to remember, then the mind may shut down because they know they cannot retain the information, but if they get continuous exposure, then the more proficient they will become and so will become relaxed and the learning will be more rapid. It is what I call **Top-Down Teaching** where the pathways in the brain are developed from the known or instinctive actions and then stimulated by the new challenges.

Although we normally think SN is about teaching the slower learner, driving difficulties are not necessarily anything to do with intelligence and may in fact be just the opposite, as lateral thinkers they may make good drivers, but it may not be conducive to passing the test. We hear of prominent celebrities who have taken many attempts to pass, but they have become perfectly capable drivers when they have been allowed to drive in their own way and when they have achieved success, they then feel able to go public about their struggles. The quick thinkers may find it more difficult to pass a set test than the pedantic plodders and denial of a problem is often a major cause of failure of the highly intelligent.

If one is academically able, it is hard to recognise one may have a diagnosable condition, so candidates with these problems are often reluctant to declare their difficulties on their Test Application. One method I use to help overcome a specific hurdle is to provide the auto where they can practise without overload. They may never have accepted driving an auto if they felt I was suggesting they had a problem and implied they could not cope with manual, but that is not how I explain it. The auto is just a ladder to assist their learning development so they accept its use without question and many choose to stay with it. They have been provided with the knowledge.

If candidates will not declare their difficulties it does mean both the instructors and the examiners will require extra skills to ensure the correct decisions are arrived at. They need to be able to **understand Hidden Difficulties as well as the Stated Disabilities.**

ix) **Theory Test Provision**

This is not the place to go into details re the would-be learners who have been prevented from actually getting to the driving test stage owing to their lack of academic prowess. We have all seen the dream taken from them, and the hope fade from their eyes, but there are a few provisions available which they can access. They rarely experience problems with HPT and usually attain high scores, but they do struggle with the MCQ where memory and language confusion are paramount. (Multiple Choice Questions)

They can book to use **Headphones** with English/Welsh read to them.

If they send a **Statement** of Educational Needs, or **EHC** (Education, Health, & Care plan), or a written **Report** by an Ed. Psychologist or Medic stating their requirements, it should be enough to enable them to receive extra time and an actual person to read the questions to them.

If they do not have any formal recognition of their need, they will require a **Letter** from their Doctor or Educational Establishment. The draw-back to just having a reader is that until recently they have only been allowed to read the question and not to explain anything, nor answer queries about the wording and this can result in misleading clues being taken from the reader. It is especially pertinent if the client struggles with Semantic Pragmatic Disorder which is an inability to understand the fine meaning of the language used in the test. So if required ask for an **Oral Language Modifier.** (where the wording can be changed). It is now available if justified.

If they have a **physical difficulty** which prevents them from holding the mouse or using the touch screen, or require wheelchair access, they can arrange to bring their own adaptation to fit to the monitor. This has to be pre-arranged and checked as not all monitors have suitable ports available.

Applying for Special Needs provision is not made easy and the booking system can be frustrating even for professional people to undertake, so if the candidate has SN, it is advisable for the ADI to book it for them, but make sure you have all relevant documentation to hand. As with all call centres your experience may be variable, but to get what your client needs you may have to insist on speaking to a Special Needs Advisor. It is usually a case of a lack of understanding as to the correct category for the client's needs, rather than the provision not being available. It can though take time.

The sifting out of would-be drivers by the MCQ has been a long standing issue since it causes problems to many of the less academic applicants and also to those who think in a different way to how the questions are worded. It **excludes** those candidates who have difficulty in studying in a logical and sequential way without becoming distracted and the instructor must be able to see beyond the **'lazy' label** with which they may have been tagged at school and which will have compounded their difficulties in trying to remember facts in isolation. In real life they are **perfectly able to understand and apply in a practical context.**

These pupils may have a vast source of information, but not be able to put it into a logical and meaningful order to answer the MCQ and these difficulties can lead to frustration and problems with self esteem which can further lead to either withdrawn or disruptive behaviour. There is a lot to overcome and a huge responsibility on ADIs and the DVSA to try to understand and address the issues to help them to succeed where formal education and driving instruction has failed them in the past.

I have taught lads under SEN who have had a deep knowledge of cars, roads and driving and what they have learnt on their own, which has stimulated their interest. They have though rejected the formal education reliant on memory, as being impossible for them to retain as many of the theory questions are. We must therefore accept **Driving Development** as the way forward in order to develop their skills at their own level and need, rather than to impose inappropriate methods and assessments from above.

ADIs who have taught those with Aspergers will appreciate their encyclopaedic knowledge of roads, transport and history and also the struggles they have to answer some of the MC Questions. On an ID section my examiner checked to see if the candidate with Aspergers had remembered the town he was supposed to be travelling toward. He immediately gave the route number he was following, even though it had never been mentioned. He knew his way, but it was not the way the examiner had given him. He had seriously struggled with the theory, but he knew it in practice. The Theory Test favours those with memory skills, but still discriminates against those who are practically knowledgeable, but whose brain may be wired differently and so struggle to access the questions.

x) **Practical Test Provision**

The DSA has always provided for those with Physical 'Special Needs', but in recent years ADIs who specialise in clients who struggle, have tried to raise an awareness of those with 'Specific Needs' in an attempt to bring the DSA in line with accepted Educational Provision and that acknowledged and provided for in the Workplace under 2010 Equality Act.-The 1981 Education Act stated that not only physical, but also learning difficulties had to be identified, recognised and provided for through legal 'Statements'. Implementation of these Statements was part of my previous career and is at the root of my deep interest in calling for the DVSA to provide for all those with Specific Needs in line with Educational practice. I believe it is now time for an independent report into the provision for all drivers with SN; not only learners, but also the increasing number of disabled drivers and those aged over seventy.

Although the recognition of Dyslexia has now become acceptable, other Specific Needs are rarely considered in Consultations and there seems to have been little understanding or provision made. Dyslexia may in fact have less effect on practical driving than other conditions.

The implementation of Independent Driving brought the whole issue of all the other Hidden Difficulties to the fore and there have been a number of cases where those with Specific Needs have been disadvantaged through the form of ID they have been asked to undertake. As far as possible, candidates should not be required to do what they would find impossible or dangerous.

Those with declared SN are allowed to choose the form of ID they would prefer and if it is thought that extra time will be required to prepare their route, they can elect for a double slot when booking. However undeclared SN are still excluded from this provision.

-'The intention of Independent Driving is not to disadvantage anyone or any element of society, to that end such a candidate may choose either ID method that best suits with any additional help. ***A candidate with Special Needs etc. can select whichever means of independent driving they would prefer.'*** (DVSA)

If candidates find reading and scanning signs difficult, they can elect for schematic diagrams; if they have sequential memory problems, then they are able to use the destination sign-reading exercise; if they struggle with both, they are allowed to make their own Post-It notes to trigger their memory, but most examiners will verbally support their memory lapses. Trials are on going to use Sat-Navs. on test for ID and as many would normally use technology, this could be a useful step forward.

As most Specific Needs are hidden, the identification of need has put an impossible responsibility on the skills of the Examiner. It is therefore the task of the ADI to make sure examiners are fully aware of the client's needs. Following a number of errors, I have negotiated with my Centre Manager to write the candidate's requirements on a card, to explain to the examiner the needs of the candidate. This would be frowned upon by some, so I would not advise it without prior authorisation of the Test Centre Manager.

The problem lies in the fact that the majority of candidates do not want to be classed as having Specific Needs, or do not have a specific diagnosis and there are others who actually object to receiving positive discrimination. It is also surprising that people having driving difficulties do not always equate it with their accepted sequential memory problems. It may be the same root, yet they presume that because they are academically capable, they will therefore not have any difficulty with driving. Of course they may not, but often they do. The examiner is then in the unenviable situation of having to determine the best way to examine their strengths, but through lack of knowledge and pressure of time they often get it wrong.

Post-It notes have been refused on the grounds of perceived danger and lack of time, so examiners prefer double slots organised at the booking stage. The simplest way is to declare 'dyspraxia' since 'dyslexia' and other Hidden Difficulties only trigger a single slot, but 'dyspraxia' is categorised as a physical problem so double time will be given for the planning.

It would help if every candidate were offered their ID preference when booking as it would remove any negative or positive discrimination whilst maintaining the integrity of the test. Why this is not acceptable has never been justified, but sometimes the simplest answer is the most difficult to effect, so my solution through information seems to be one way forward.

xi) **How do YOU respond?**

Many readers will have bought this book after having read my previous ones which went into more detail regarding teaching ideas and specific successes; but I also realise that some will be considering these matters for the first time and that the comments I have made may be regarded as quite revolutionary or outside the parameters suggested in your training. There will be others who have been questioning, **'is there another way?'** but have wondered if it would be acceptable and what it should be: of-course that depends on the development of your personal skills as a teacher and the relationship between you and your individual students.

Some new instructors would regard their job to be working to a set syllabus to train learners to perform in the way they would act, until hopefully, they turned into replicas of themselves. It therefore comes as quite a surprise when a number of their trainees don't learn that way and they wonder why. Just as we cannot tell our trainees how to drive independently, no one can tell the teacher how to teach independently. It is not dependent on academic study or a set course or philosophy since the skills you require are not only client specific, but will **change during each lesson**. The key question to ask is whether both you and your students are succeeding and enjoying the lessons, since many learners are pushed into traditional forms of instruction which overwhelm them. **If they are not succeeding or enjoying the lessons then something needs addressing.**

One aspect of my work is to re-train drivers following brain injury and the problems they encounter are very similar to those that our learners with hidden difficulties experience. There may be some part of the brain which does not operate in quite the same way as we would expect, but exciting research into brain function is revealing more and more about how the brain can seek out new pathways and directions in order to cope with the problems and begin to work adequately again. Until recently the concept that one could learn to see by using other senses such as the touch or hearing would have seemed to be science fiction, so we should not dismiss our candidates who struggle, but rather seek out exciting and creative ways to help them to succeed.

There may be another pathway for them if only we can discover it.

The more experience I have had as a Driving Instructor, the more I have observed the vast differences in drivers' skill, aptitude, attitude, experience, health, perception, reaction speed, and the ability to predict and problem-solve. I realised that irrespective of intelligence or education, many drivers do not see or do what I would think was common sense; not deliberately or because of stupidity or road rage, but because they do not perceive the situation in the way I do, or have the experience to predict, or the ability to find the same solutions.

The skill level of some of our candidates may not be as brilliant as others, but we can still help them to compensate by teaching 'care' for others, awareness and defensive driving whilst exposing them to many wider experiences. The serious accidents on our roads are not usually caused by those with problems, but by those whose attitude is poor, or who believe they are highly skilled. It is therefore also necessary to educate our naturally skilled drivers to understand that they need to allow more time for drivers who are less skilled than they are.

As part of Pass Plus I encourage my higher skilled drivers to experience driving with hand controls as it teaches them to be more aware of the hidden needs of others who share the road with them. All strands of society are on our roads and all drivers need to be taught to be aware of and to accept each other's needs. There has to be a place for all, rather than just those who fit a pre-determined standard, at a given time, on a given day.

As part of the development of your work as an instructor I would encourage all readers to research further into the three conditions covered in this book. I have only just touched upon the spectrums and there are of course many other **neurological diversities** and hidden difficulties we may encounter which do not fit the standard teaching template. Some may be temporary and caused by trauma which if given time and the required help the brain can heal. We must not 'write them off', but instead try as many different ways as possible to help them achieve the same as those we teach whom we would regard as being 'normal.' If you decide to specialise in this area of work you will not be disappointed as it is both fascinating and extremely rewarding, **when you see lives changed because of your interest, care, knowledge and developing expertise.** *John P Brown 2016*